Poetry by Dennis O'Driscoll

KIST

HIDDEN EXTRAS

LONG STORY SHORT

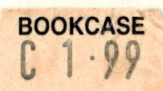
Dennis O'Driscoll

QUALITY TIME

ANVIL PRESS POETRY

Published in 1997
by Anvil Press Poetry Ltd
Neptune House 70 Royal Hill London SE10 8RT

This book is published with financial assistance
from The Arts Council of England

Set in Bembo by Anvil Press Poetry
Printed and bound in England
by Morganprint (Blackheath) Ltd

ISBN 0 85646 290 X

A catalogue record for this book
is available from the British Library

FOR NICHOLAS TWIST
AND
PATRICIA MOLLOY

I once
had
a plan

I would build
a million-span bridge
to the sun

Alone
out of that dream
survives

the foundation stone

lodged
in
my heart

(after MAK DIZDAR)

ACKNOWLEDGEMENTS

Acknowledgements are due to the following publications where some of these poems previously appeared: *Agenda, Atlanta Review, Cobweb, Columbia, Crab Orchard Review, Harvard Review, Irish Times, New England Review, The North, Poetry Ireland Review, Poetry London Newsletter, Poetry Review, Sibila, Southern Review, Sunday Business Post, Sunday Tribune, Verse.* 'Customs' was first published in *Poetry* (Chicago).

'The Bottom Line' was published in a limited edition by The Dedalus Press, Dublin, 1994.

CONTENTS

PART ONE

YOU

Be yourself: show your flyblown eyes
to the world, give no cause for concern,
wash the paunchy body whose means you
live within, suffer the illnesses
that are your prerogative alone –

the prognosis refers to nobody but you;
you it is who gets up every morning
in your skin, you who chews your dinner
with your mercury-filled teeth, gaining
garlic breath or weight, you dreading,

you hoping, you regretting, you interloping.
The earth has squeezed you in, found you space;
any loss of face you feel is solely yours –
you with the same old daily moods, debts,
intuitions, food fads, pet hates, Achilles' heels.

You carry on as best you can the task of being,
whole-time, you; you in wake and you in dream,
at all hours, weekly, monthly, yearly, life,
full of yourself as a tallow candle is of fat,
wallowing in self-denial, self-esteem.

THE NIGHT WATCH

I answer the door
to wasps.
A dawn chorus,
vibrato humming,
sheer wings
quivering in the dark.
A Biblical swarm.
Landing, flying,
increasing, multiplying.
Primed cluster bombs.
A sizzling pan.
A holiday traffic jam.
A battle dance:
taunting, sizing up
the enemy, ready
to bayonet-charge
with stings.
A Bombay slum,
car horns, scooters,
cries of limbless beggars.
Stalactites of venom.
Gossips. Looters.
Refugees massed
on a platform
wailfully resisting
their fate.
A nervous spasm.
A panic fit.
The engine goes on
revving up for action,
a blistering
multi-pronged attack.
The star-coated sky
is˙blacked out
by the throng.

LAST FLIGHT

I

Winter frosts
kill off the wasps
who had escaped
the sticky end
of the jam-jar trap,
its sweet watery grave.

The hive in the roof
is too big now
for those few still alive,
old crippled nuns
in the cold cells
of a redundant convent.

II

A lone survivor protrudes from the grout.
No vigour left in limb or wing.
To spare it pain, I stub it out.
O wasp, where is thy sting?

SELLING OUT

I

We contracted to sell the lot.
The angle of attack of heavy rain.
The bedroom with the rising damp spot.
The dawn shunt of a gypsum train.
The night creak of boards, metallic pings.
The tree fungi like heaped-up plates.
The valedictory spider tying strings.
Swivel press. Clothes-line. Blackbirds in spate.

II

When the sparrow tilted the balance of the pear tree.
When the apples were setting out their stalls.
When the scaly sea sparkled like a fizzy drink.
When the yew thirsted for the juices of the moon.
When your lavender deck chair sprawled
near the gangly hollyhocks.
When the palm tree – so alienated all winter –
fanned itself against premeditated heat.
When the robin came within two feet of your wellingtons.
When the neighbours were away.
When stamens bowed with gold dust.
When rust had yet to blight the lilacs.
When the white of the indecisive butterfly
was like the surface on a bowl of double cream.
When you returned upstairs
and stole a last glance at the view.
When you found the sky had misted over.
When the deed was done.

LIGHTING UP TIME

for Patrick Taylor

I

Rites of spring: roll out
your hibernating lawnmower,
dead grass wedged to blades;
line up the cans of paint,
sandpaper, brushes, rags.

II

The cottage garden
in the mauve light
of delphiniums.
Lilies with honeyed tongues.

Bird notes tossed
like blossoms.
A fern stretching
its wings.

III

Vulcanised rubber snails,
plump as a colony of seals,
make the viscous journey
to a meal of hosta leaves.

IV

Those daffodils,
you'd know it was
their first time:

so open, so eager to please,
so bright, so upright,
so unaware.

V

The raw nerve of yearning
triggered by hawthorn,
by the green of far-off hills
seen from your top-floor office
when sun pays out its light.

VI

That it might
always be spring,
a held note.

That we might
look forward
to long days

of growth:
haze lifting
like a screen,

waves peeling
off the Gulf Stream
one by one.

CUSTOMS

A small airport. A plane
lost in a fog of thought
    like a train nettle-deep
    in a siding. It has seen
mountain tops streaked with zebra
skins of snow, fields like cracks
    on an Old Master landscape,
    flickering cities – buried
treasure – through snagged clouds.

Early arrivals delayed,
the girl at the Hertz desk
    jokes with the passport clerk.
    A cleaner leans on his mop.
And the control tower
rising from the mist
    like a border look-out
    sets the Customs official
off on a reverie of his own,

when the weight of January snow
buckled the roof on his
    solitary outpost; kicking stones
    along the byroad in July
– a tractor armed to cut hay
would bring a moment of diversion:
    as its engine dwindled, the stream
    could be heard more clearly,
the grass growing under his feet.

BORDER POSTS

Pettigo and Kilclean.
Kildrum Mobile and Muff.
Scuttled by the single market.
Hulls of prefabs left to rot.

The redeployed Customs staff,
bored, trying to acclimatise
themselves to indoor jobs, perk up
at a mention of the names.

Nights on cattle-truck surveillance.
Swerving at high speed through boreens.
Bomb scares. Videos, spirits, derv.
The CPO. The local girls. The cards.

PARTING

I

the abandoned look of tracks
under a twinkling frost

criss-crossing at a junction
then going their separate ways

parallel rails
converging in infinity

which once bore trains
that ran on time

II

the ghetto diary lurches
to a sudden halt

a mystery train's brakes
screeching at a destination

of smokestacks and raked hair:
gaze next at blank endpapers

where the narrative continues
on parchment skin, thin air

READING THE SIGNS

The ebbing tints of a winter evening
fall on walls, tower blocks, cobblestones,
tall statues of The Leader in his metal
greatcoat, tombs of soldiers known, unknown.

For a while the grandeur of old sooty buildings
is restored, architraves glow like coals,
and a doleful queue for rumoured pork
is transfixed by amethyst and gold.

The man at the office window stands
for a moment in the encroaching gloom
before he checks for electricity and finds
a margarine light coveting his stark room.

A flat at the peak of a serpentine staircase:
young Literary Circle writers take the floor
under dusty plaster mouldings and peeled paint
to risk new poems, a typed *Nineteen Eighty-Four*;

now, in brighter days, they can relax
at the outdoor restaurant near the tramline,
sun-dappled tables beside blossoming apple trees.
The *plat de jour* of giblets will need time

but they are free to wait; an editor –
still furtive from old habits – starts to pass
his latest publication round, reading the future
when blossoms float down to his Coca-Cola glass.

UNDYING

from birth our countdown begins
muffled with heartbeats

    ★

at what stage does the dying start
at what point do you decide
it is not worth renewing the subscription
that it will be up to your successors
to repair the bathroom lock

    ★

what a waste
to create such radiance
then pitch it – body and soul – away
heat so unlike death
breath so sweet

    ★

marble is not the proper way
to enshrine her memory
whose name looks cold in stone
whose flesh creased with the least pressure

    ★

sans everything but mind
a mind alert to its collapsing shell

as if a child had intimations
of mortality and could foretell

the circumstances of his death
wise to the world he would be weaned from

*

let her come back
let her rekindle love
as she set morning fires
the dated newspaper
evaporating with flame

*

the doctor confirms your own diagnosis
a smell of sickness
sniffed already like damp air

*

let's suppose we die
let's suppose they bury us like bulbs
let's suppose we rot rather than flower
let's suppose we are not punished or saved
let's suppose time and space are infinite
let's suppose life happens only once
let's suppose we die

*

for as long as blood–oxygen
sprinkles your brain
and your mouth waters with life

*

the unborn grow restive with delays
they need our room, our food
they have destinies to fulfil
their passion fuels our desires

*

we wanted to hold
on to our dead
to mourn them
when we felt the need

like pets caged
inside coffins
to be released
for exercise, fresh air

*

inconceivable they
could be forgotten:
then our lives were
rearranged like chairs

their set places
at our dining tables
and in our minds
were lost

we had let them die

WATER

The miracle of water
is that it tastes of nothing,
neither of chlorine nor peat,
not of old tap fittings or dead sheep.

Water was the first mirror,
drinking images of beauty,
showing their wrinkled future
in the mildest breeze.

Water clings to its neutrality,
changes state at boiling point,
finds the level at which
tensions cool, limbs relax.

It is the splinter of ice in the heart,
the white blood of the snowman,
the burst main flooding
from Christ's frozen side.

HALLOWEEN

(on my mother's 70th birthday)

Summer is saved,
rolled up in carpets
of straw and hay,
    folded away
    like picnic chairs.
Autumn dusks try out
rose, mauve, magenta
brushstrokes of sky
    like celestial light
    poking through
the clouds in holy pictures
or rays squirting
from the thorn-pierced
    sacred heart
    above our parents' bed
(six of us sentenced to life
there in that room).
Under a marble headboard,
    sedated by her pneuma,
    does she watch out for a sign?
I tug at a dandelion
whose milky root
unravels underground;
    I smooth the coverlet
    of gravel that might be
made of goosebumps;
shuddering suddenly, she'd say:
Someone's walking on my grave.

SUN SPOTS

A hazy dawning.
The jogger's trainers
stained by dewy grass.

Midges mix and mingle.
Morning clears its throat
through a cock's crow.

A horse grows from sleep
to full height,
kick-starts into life.

I shut out the news,
gag the car stereo's mouth
with a Purcell ode.

And sun triumphs in the end
– resplendent, brassy, baroque –
trumpeting the day.

★

Summer's warmth falters
to a cube of tawny light,
a stage where Chekhov is performed.

By now, the lavish stretch in the evenings
that prompted bus-stop conversation
has been squandered.

Isobars tighten like layers of clothes.
The year is an off-season dacha,
ready for boarding-up,

a play in which a band
is made out in the distance,
marching away. Wafting. Fading.

*And time will pass
and we shall be forgotten:
our faces, our voices, our pain.*

★

The momentary glint of tin,
the flash in the pan,
has remained precious this long,

long enough for the still-life
painter's name to be unknown,
wiped out like flesh and bone,

like the bruised fruits
(liver plums, skull pears)
the viewers stalk

with hungry eyes,
ripe for the simple truths
the sun bares,

making light of water,
pinpointing
the pitcher's soul.

THE ONE TWENTY PUB

after Wisława Szymborska

The bomb is primed to go off at one twenty.
A time-check: one sixteen.
There's still a chance for some to join
the pub's ranks, for others to drop out.

The terrorist watches from across the street.
Distance will shield him
from the impact of what he sees:

A woman, turquoise jacket on her shoulder,
enters; a man with sunglasses departs.
Youths in tee-shirts loiter without intent.
One seventeen and four seconds.
The scrawny motorcyclist, revving up
to leave, won't believe his luck;
but the tall man steps straight in.

One seventeen and forty seconds.
That girl, over there with the walkman
– now the bus has cut her off.
One eighteen exactly.
Was she stupid enough to head inside?
Or wasn't she? We'll know before long,
when the dead are carried out.

It's one nineteen.
Nothing much to report
until a muddled barfly hesitates,
fumbles with his pockets and, like
a blasted fool, stumbles back
at one nineteen and fifty seconds
to retrieve his goddamned cap.

One twenty.
How time drags when...
Any moment now.
Not yet.
Yes.
    Yes,
        there
            it
                goes.

SIN

grant us sin, O Lord
we need to believe in sin
in the halo of pain

rising from caned buttocks
the body and blood savoured
in the beads of sudden jism

we need to believe it is wrong
to anoint each other with our chrism
as if lives depended on this

we need to believe it is wicked
to eavesdrop at the peak-hour rate
on cheap recordings of bored wives

do not forgive us, O Lord
our sense of emptiness after the event
our hollow cries of pleasure, woe

spice with a heightened shame
the slow ritual of removing vestments
the awe with which hands tremble

in the presence of transient flesh
that even to the naked eye
is Your own image and likeness

teach us to treat sweet secret passages
as dens of iniquity and filth
when, guilty and abashed,

we turn back to Your clasp

PIONEERS

for Olga Kelly and Tom Sheedy

How did we stand it?
Our squat bungalows plonked down
in the middle of a muddy field,
unfinished and unadorned.

Everything was unprecedented, strange,
edged with an expectant silence.
Pick and spade to hand, I manfully
staked my pride on an undulating lawn...

The house was ours; ours the pressured
water snarling from its taps; ours
the otherworldly quiet of its attic ribcage,
neat and insulated as a chaffinch nest.

Light fell gently on us sometimes,
gasping at the beauty of a morning glass
of orange juice, scooping a chute of sun
that dusted our sparse furniture with warmth,

finding its way to dew-sprayed lettuce
left by our good neighbours on the sill.
Next to the rubbish infill at the roundabout,
the precast concrete of the industrial estate:

forklifts, palettes, cameras, crates,
slavering guard dogs; wildflowers swept
clay ramparts under lumpy yellow carpets.
Environs so Iron Curtain, so consigned

to squalor, shoddiness and grot,
that when our poet-friend had finally
identified our nameless street,
Hello there, Comrades was his opening shot.

THE NEXT POEM

My next poem is quite short and it's about something most of you will recognise. It came out of an experience I had on holidays a couple of years ago. In fact, I'm pretty sure I'm correct in saying that it's the only poem I've ever managed to write during my holidays, if you could have called this a holiday – it bore all the hallmarks of an endurance test.

There's a reference in the poem to roller canaries, which become more or less mythical birds in the last line. I hope the context will make that clear. Incidentally, this poem has gone down extremely well in Swedish translation – which maybe reveals a bit about *me!* A word I'd better gloss is 'schizont'; if I can locate the slip of paper, I'll give you the dictionary definition. Yes, here we are: 'a cell formed from a trophozoite during the asexual stage of the life cycle of protozoans of the class *Sporozoa*'.

OK then, I'll read this and just two or three further sequences before I finish. By the way, I should perhaps explain that the title is in quotations. It's something I discovered in a book on early mosaics; I wanted to get across the idea of diversity and yet unity at the same time, especially with an oriental, as it were, orientation. And I need hardly tell this audience which of my fellow-poets is alluded to in the phrase 'dainty mountaineer' in the second section. Anyway, here it is. Oh, I nearly forgot to mention that the repetition of the word 'nowy' is deliberate. As I said, it's quite short. And you have to picture it set out on the page as five sonnet-length trapezoids. Here's the poem.

THERE AND THEN

and there they are
leaning over the bridge
figures from childhood
as if waiting all their lives
for my return

*

evenings damp and vacant
            as underground caves
the smoky boredom
            permeating winter Sundays
the litter-swirling emptiness
            after a hurling game
teachers and bank clerks adjourning
            to the club-house bar

*

I am out on the isthmus of school holidays
nesting in a bolstered tea-chest
feeding on two Lone Pine books a day

*

granted one cloudless afternoon
crowds walked from town with towels
and tractor tubes to swim this river
as you tried to memorise
the Gallic Wars from a curled page

*

there is no end to this lane
in sight: look at the light
off in the distance

you would need to be young
to negotiate this gate
to run the gauntlet

of reminiscent greenness
saturating all sides
a corridor between two lives

★

blackcurrant bushes that ripened
in your youth bear fruit still

you could check them out this minute
remind yourself how memory tastes

look back through sleek black pupils
at summers picking them for jam

★

a childhood illness
the starched stillness of the bedroom
an anxious mother tapping out pills

★

the road I draw
is the one outside our door
it leads to mass, infants' class
Kilroy's toyshop, my cousins' farm

I am putting everything I have
into this picture
biting my tongue with concentration

clock hands join above the church
square-wheeled trucks haul sugar beet
a polka-dotted friesian strays
out of my farm set

for no reason at all
I add a big round steamroller:
now maybe I will win the prize

★

that orchard was the last green fastness
glossy cooking apples, dock leaves, moss

cows, horses, goats, fleecy cauliflowers of sheep
two by two they grazed the flood-prone fields

wood smoke, gas lamps, willow pattern, deal
bellows, wholemeal bread, fuchsia sprigs

★

and so much has disappeared
digging up your roots
bulldozing fields
where you knew every clover tassel
every thistle spike

★

not just the way the dead fade
but also how the living
vanish into the living

dust off that face which greets
you in the street to find
beneath the carapace of age

the thigh-baring beauty
which scorched itself
into your very bones

place your fingers in the names
chiselled on your parents' tombstones
to believe that they once lived

and cared enough to part hair
floss teeth
choose your first communion suit

    *

a few of us were making for home
finished our Legion of Mary visits

walking or taking our time on bicycles
wobbling along at the speed of speech:

as the church clock counted twelve
streetlights switched off

like a lapse of memory
and darkness was declared

FAITH, HOPE, LOSS

1. I stumble on you, prostrate by the door, flat out in a frenzied search for a dropped ear-ring or stone, as if vowing to reform your life in exchange for the recovery of the trinket.

2. With mounting helplessness and rage, my route is retraced in my mind, until I suspect it was in the airport phone booth that I left the missing bag.

3. Losing a loved one. Seeing a daughter eviscerated by cancer, her kindly discoloured face beneath the numbered hairs.

4. To be one of the world's 5.7 billion people: reaching climax, anaesthetised with blockbusters and booze, delving in bins for found art, discarded food. Or one of the three unique species annihilated every hour as grasslands, open-cast mines, weekend shacks impinge.

5. The ditch of lisping water laced with greens, awash with swaying tendrils, dunked leaves, is cemented over; spring light of primroses extinguished; slashed briars where a robin summed up April dusks.

6. Bliss consists of the smallest things. The bus already there to meet the all-night train. Unhappiness lies in what we miss.

7. You are on your knees, convinced that what seems irredeemably lost continues to exist, keeping faith that – given time and patience – it will be restored.

NON ISSUE

Our new car, stopping at
the lollipop lady's command,
is bought with money saved
from the expense of children.
And this restaurant meal
is possible because
there are no other
mouths to feed.

This brass bedstead was acquired
through denying ransom
to the unborn children
who demand our money
and our life.
That antique tallboy came
from their pocket money,
wall-hangings from college fees.

These pre-concert snorters
are equivalent in cost
to babysitter or au pair;
and this free love
we can make is safe
from bawling children,
smalls littered on the floor
as in an adolescent's room.

SONG

At Creevykeel

The sun climbs,
A cuckoo spreads its charms,
Limpid blobs of dew
Bind newly-minted grass
On the early-morning farms.

We follow a plot of death
But not to keen or whine
At this ancient 'giant's grave'
Where a cuckoo warms up
While the sun shines.

Death is an obsolete rite,
A shard of carbon-dated bone,
Remote to us who stray here –
Fresh from bed and breakfast –
As this cairn of skeletal stone.

The cuckoo chants.
Lambs bounce on springy feet.
The first fly of the year
Sweeps through a cottage window.
The day is gathering heat

At Creevykeel.

VARIATIONS FOR WIND

When a wind like this is blowing, it somehow comes home to you
that man has been flung into the world.

ANDREI SINYAVSKY

I

Forget the gentle zephyr of legend,
the washday breeze dislodging suds

like cherry blossom from the line,
the therapeutic music of wind

at a bellows-driven, pine-crackling fire…
Whipped up by a cloud-furrowed

brooding sky, gusts lick the eaves
like flame, swig from window glass:

a hurricane crescendo drowning
naked cries, a day of judgement

as you rise from sleep to Gods
whom neither winds nor seas obey.

II

Think in terms of hiding
as storms hit their winter stride.

Raw wind gnaws your ears;
turn the other cheek,

turn from the foam-streaked sea
to the haven of the pub.

Knock back a hot whiskey,
discard the sopping anorak.

Keep your eyes peeled
for anyone in the room you know.

Through a headstrong plume
of cigarettes, begin counting days.

III

Sang-froid. The way the bird
would tune up every dawn.

Something set it going
like a car alarm; all through

atonal January, the strident
woodwind of the gales,

it tried to stave off harm
as though by scaling high notes

it could stop the flexing
cypress limbs it perched on

from toppling down upon us
in the next aggressive gust.

IV

You must leave – today, not tomorrow –
the face behind the ticket kiosk

seems to say. It's an ill wind
that blows: if not a Venetian sirocco,

the plutonium breeze ripping through
bilge-thickened seas, a *force*

majeure throwing spores of
incaution to the winds. The sewage

boat discharges filmy cargo,
like crude oil, off beaches

where Tadzios paddled
in gold stoneground sand.

V

That we will come,
ultimately, to nothing

– this the wind ensures,
threatening to break and enter,

binding black fumes of cloud
around the rheum-eyed moon;

and you start to understand,
looking out at where umbrellas

struggle like the bony wings
of prehistoric birds,

this planet is not habitable;
streets are paved with silver rain.

VI

Yes, we do have homes to go to
when the nights are cold and drab,

places we can be ourselves in,
universal potholed streets

along which someone scurries
through the shadows always,

the inlaid gem of a cigarette
above his leather jacket, jeans.

You sink into the fireside chair
that has assumed your very contours,

outstare the fangs of coal a wind
is taunting, buff your muddy shoes.

VII

A churning, stomach-turning,
seasick sea: a gothic scene

as, once again, rain-clouds –
ragged curtains – lacerate the moon.

Waves gasp ashore, collapse,
unload their concave burdens

and, sieved through shingle,
pour off surplus water on dry land,

rub salt into the wounded air.
Seas somewhere harbour warmer

colours, weathered copper melding
into verdigris. Azure.

VIII

After winter, like a chronic illness,
has kept up its tired routine,

the analeptic light which you
aspire to will strike soon

out of the blue: creepers stir
from purdah, decked with

festive blooms, butterflies
rise like the jubilant flags

of a liberated archipelago,
yellow flowers baste tall grass.

You recall how wild the roses smell
when doused by summer showers...

ALL

all journeying together
the living and the dead
all that are alive
all that will be dead
all that will be born
all that ever lived
remains accompany us
like meteorites
husks of dead bees
tusks of dead elephants
mandibles of termites
snouts of seahorses
spouts of whales
necks of giraffes
not a speck of moth's
dust is mislaid
wings of bluebottles
stings of scorpions
suction pads of leeches
gill chambers of fish
species certified
extinct on shale
still dwell among us
as alive once
as the neighbours
of our own future graves
who pass us daily
on the teeming streets

DECEMBER

That evening at the far end of the year, I was drafting a staff guide to the new Regulation. Gerry, stirring his tankard of tea, was responding to some Transit query on the telephone. Maurice's fountain pen, as usual, was in full flow, goaded by the demon of deadlines. All of us vaguely aware of the sun setting feverishly at our shoulders. One minute, its extravagance resembled the Caribbean postcard taped to the filing cabinet; the next, it was a lurid plate out of an illustrated Dante.

Our Christmas party would take place later. The air was taut with anticipation. Gerry split a packet of Rich Tea biscuits and sighed for his dancing days. Showbands striking a chord with 'O Darling!…'. Dimmed lights, distempered halls… The last plash of sunset, an abstract colour-field canvas, sharpened the outlines of buildings, the vertebrae of cranes stooped over the tax-incentive area nearby.

We lapsed back into another pen-scratched silence then. It would be a great night. A tree twitched off and on. Someone keyed-out on the corridor. The church steeples looked pathetic from our level – so small and helpless, jabbing at the dark.

TIME CHECK

To tell the hour, you need
an old-style wind-up wall-clock
swinging the lead of its pendulum,
marching in time with the seconds,
a child keeping step with a parade;

the sound of time when – too engrossed
to notice – we let it pass us by
or when it punctuates the silence
a lovers' tiff fomented, each moment
a drip of Chinese water-torture.

In the aftermath of a death,
the pendulum is stilled: a heart
snatched in a coroner's gloved hand;
released later, a pulsating fish,
the flicked blades of its fins

slicing through shaded streams.
Time must be heard no less than seen
as it goes around in circles.
A girl anticipates her first menses,
her harassed mother her last;

a dog barks from a distant farm
all through the vigil of a sleepless night...
The clock rations out your seconds,
checks them off, tots them up aloud.
Then its trance-inducing pendulum asks

for your childhood back, your life.

SUCCESS STORY

Your name is made.
You have turned the company around,
downsized franchise operations,
increased market penetration
on the leisure side,
returned the focus to core business.
Man of the Month in the export journal,
ruffler of feathers, raiser of dust,
at the height of your abilities.

You don't suspect it yet, but from now on
it will be gradually downhill.
This year or the next you will
barely notice any change – your tan offsets
the thinning of your blow-dried hair,
you recharge your batteries
with longer weekend snooze-ins,
treat back trouble with heat pad and massage,
install an ergonomic chair for daytime comfort.

Behind closed boardroom doors
there will be talk: not quite
the man you were, losing your grip,
ideas a bit blah, in danger
of becoming a spent force.
To your astonishment, the question
of an early severance package comes up
delicately over coffee, low-key as
'Can you pass the sugar, please?'

The flamboyant young blood you trained
starts to talk down, to interrupt
half-way through your report
on grasping brassplate opportunities.
You hear yourself say *In my day*
more often than you should.
Bite your tongue.
Brighten your tie.
Show your old readiness to fight.

TALKING SHOP

What does it profit a man to own the poky
grocery shop he sleeps above, unlocking at eight,
not stopping until some staggeringly late hour?

Even before opening, he has driven his van
to the market, replenished supplies of bananas,
apples – nothing too exotic for local demand.

Seven days, he takes his place behind formica,
the delights of his mother's age preserved
in shelves of jelly, custard, sago pudding.

Peaches on his waterlogged display outside
will still be smarting from the previous day's
rain as though steeped in their own juice,

cabbage-leaves prismatic with drops.
A propped radio brings up-to-the-minute news
or, in slack periods, he reviews things

at first hand, standing sentry in the doorway,
watching nobody come or go from the plain-
faced cottages opposite: once they unleashed

mid-morning shoppers; now wives work,
supermarkets supply all but a few spontaneous
needs: shoelaces, low-fat milk, shampoo.

Finally, the shutter is wound down again,
the life he leads is his business exclusively.
Perpetual light shines on the tiny cash box.

You will see for yourself, through the slats,
the rows of cans like tin hats, suits of armour,
maybe hoarded as a foretaste of impending war.

THEM AND YOU

They wait for the bus.
You spray them with puddles.

They queue for curry and chips.
You phone an order for delivery.

They place themselves under the protection
of the Marian Grotto at the front of their estate.

You put your trust in gilts, managed funds,
income continuation plans.

They look weathered.
You look tanned.

They knock back pints.
You cultivate a taste for vintage wines.

They get drunk.
You get pleasantly inebriated.

Their wives have straw hair.
Yours is blonde.

They are missing one football card
to complete the full set.

You keep an eye out for a matching
Louis XV-style walnut hall table.

They are hoping for a start with a builder.
You play your part in the family firm.

They use loose change, welfare coupons.
You tap your credit card impatiently on the counter.

They lean over the breeze-block wall to gossip.
You put down motions for the Residents' AGM.

They have a hot tip for Newmarket.
You have the inside track on a rights issue.

They go over the top.
You reach it.

They preach better pay.
You practise it.

VOYAGER

I

The weight of sadness escaping like a gas,
like a vapour of doleful music from the radio's
capsule, defying the airiness of spring,
out of tune with bluebells, streaked tulips,
wet lilac reek, lewd boys crushing
the strawberry lips of their colluding girls.

II

The boating holiday we'd planned to treat
him to: sedge and reed-beds; willows trailing
slender arms in water, as if from a skiff;
calm evenings with reading light till ten
when mayflies tantalise the slurping lake,
sun comes filtered through a sieve of leaves.

III

He will live a little longer: death
signs clarify like the stars that filled
his x-ray vision one night on a mountain
as eyes adapted to the dark; ground lightning
launched distress flares and he stared
inconclusively into the sky's black hole.

IV

Rocks, lock gates, whirlpools, tidal flows:
his fingers trace the mapped obstacles faced
between the river's origin and the cold,
salt-preserved finality of sea, cut water
healing in his wake while he rows, as though
for dear life, towards the beating sun.

BREVIARY

The Cow
   after K. Schippers

The cow
is a funny artiste:
whatever the beast
has in mind
it always comes out
as a moo.

   ★

Winter Haiku

men in women's shops
   women sizing up men's clothes
portents of Christmas

   ★

Postbox

a mystical moment when
having held it in suspension
checked it front and back
ensured the stamp is firmly glued
you let the letter go

   ★

Oven Ready

a headless corpse
in a plastic bag
neck driven like a rivet
up its behind

remove transplanted organs
from the ribbed crypt
rinse the body
naked pink newborn

★

Off-duty

reclining in the garden overnight
your deck chair soaking up the moonlight

★

Trunk Road

I
hug
you like
a tree which
stands in the way
of a planned new road.
I throw my arms around you
like a protestor who will not
let the tree be felled, whose vigil
is silhouetted against dusk, while night
etches in bulldozers, trucks, blunt instruments
of
death.

★

Still Life

a spongeware bowl
in leaf-and-berry motif
smoulders with nectarines
hot coals

★

Home

when all is said and done
what counts is having someone
you can phone at five to ask

for the immersion heater
to be switched to 'bath'
and the pizza taken from the deepfreeze

PART TWO
The Bottom Line

[1]

Official standards, building regulations,
fair procedures for dismissing errant staff:
my brain is crammed with transient knowledge
– patent numbers, EC directives, laws.
I pause at traffic lights on the way back
to headquarters; windscreen wipers skim off
visions of this seeping stone-faced town:
a warehouse frontage littered with crates,
lovers locked in an umbrella-domed embrace,
consumers at a bank dispenser drawing cash.
I race the engine, inch the car towards green.

[2]

The kind of suit a man of this age
must wear: single or double-breasted,
turn-ups – or not – on the trousers,
usual lapels; the right space between
the blue stripes of monogrammed shirts...
Problems which preoccupy me now, struggling
with pre-meeting notes, will pass away
like fashions: funny collars, ties
my grandchildren can scoff at, looking down
on forebears when, marking some anniversary,
the blanched album does the rounds.

[3]

Quality time at weekends, domestic bliss:
early pathways cordoned off by webs,
I slip out to the shops, return
to bring you tea and newspapers in bed.
On Sundays, every Sunday, I submit to the calm
of supplements, CDs, cooking smells.
All of the mornings of all the weekdays
I leave for work; my office bin fills
with the shredded waste of hours.
A pattern regular as wallpaper or rugs
and no more permanent than their flowers.

[4]

Anxieties you could elevate
to the level of a mid-life crisis
are mere reactions to your dreary days,
the boss's ire, tiresome assignments.
You scan the pink financial pages
on the way home, nodding off and on,
jaded, blinking at suburban nameplates
with each juddering halt the train makes.
Wives are parked by railings, silhouettes
of baby seats; a mumbled greeting, then
you unwind to family anecdotes, TV.

[5]

I am a trustworthy, well-adjusted citizen
at this stage, capable of a commanding
pungency in business talk, good grasp
of office jargon, the skill to rest
phones on my shoulders as I keep tabs,
the ability to clinch a deal convincingly...
I recognise a counterpart when our paths
cross in sandwich bar or jazz shop and we nod
to each other with a telling smile, maybe
recall negotiations where we held opposing lines,
all discreet charm now, agendas agreed.

[6]

A life of small disappointments, hardly
meriting asperity or rage, a fax
sent to the wrong number, an engagement
missed, a client presentation failing
to persuade: nothing you can't sweat off
at gym or squash. But, in the dark filling
of the night, doubts gather with the rain
which, spreading as predicted from the west,
now leaves its mark on fuscous window panes;
and you wait for apprehensions to dissolve
in the first glimmer of curtain light.

[7]

Pressing tanned flesh, reaching consensus
over some outstanding fact, our well-
scrubbed, nail-filed hands feel soft.
Enough contact with the soil is made
weeding invasive seedlings from the lawn...
Best of all, undo the crested tie,
change into fawn slacks and turtle-neck,
white-fringed golfing shoes, commune
with nature between fairway and rough,
taking the air on a bracing Saturday
or sharing honours for the captain's prize.

[8]

When you unclasp your slimline briefcase,
the apple, deep green, high gloss
with waxen sheen, a tea-break snack,
glows among the acetate reports,
symbolising something you can't name
but crave for when your sales, morale
are low − peace, a meaningful existence...
You settle for a rental in the west,
family away-days, the company car,
and, who can tell, later you may rise
to a weekend cottage, hens, a bright-red door.

[9]

How did I get this far, become
this worldly-wise, letting off steam
to suppliers, sure of my own ground?
What did my dribbling, toddling stage
prepare me for? What was picked up
from cloth-paged books, stuffed bears,
all those cute gap-toothed years?
So embarrassing the idiocies of my past,
seen from the vantage of tooled-leather
and buffed teak, hands-on management
techniques, line logistics, voice mail.

At the visitors' car park, the belts
of our trench coats flap with the wind;
we huddle in a confidential group
hoping to have pressed home the point,
a hollow Coke can tinkling on the street.
Then, despite this meeting of minds,
for one long second we run out of things
to say, permit thoughts chill as downturns
to stray into our heads until we contrive
the next move, check watch or schedule,
arrange matters arising, part on a jocose note.

[11]

Photos of my family – wife and sons –
framed in silver near my conference phone
inspire me to seize every chance I get,
make life better for the children
as my parents – sweat of the brow
and all that – did for me; my spouse
is most supportive, clued into the dog-
eat-dog mentality success requires.
Ferrying the kids to school in style
imbues them in the long term with
some gainful aspirations of their own.

[12]

Pay day, the carefree junior staff
stroll back from the bank, flush with
spending power, indulging in the luxury
of ice-cream, crisps; a typist, due to
rejoin soon, lifts her baby like a trophy,
weighs with friends the pros and cons
of a career break... It is the wider
picture I rake over in my mind: how
gearing can improve; whether to draw
the blind on loss-making subsidiaries
and let the liquidator worry about debts.

[13]

The hidden pain of offices: a mission
statement admonishing me from walls,
the volatility of top brass if sales volume
for a single line falls one per cent.
And customers' righteousness, their touching
faith in the perfectibility of man.
Yet even without the big compensations
– personalised number plates, offshore
tax breaks – I enjoy the hectic pace;
and when, spaced-out, I have an off-day,
I spend my way back to normality.

[14]

All this stuff here I've worked hard
to own, installed alarms to keep,
could disappear tomorrow at the hands
of some dumb creep in shiny track-suit,
a suede-headed galoot out on bail...
Such negative conclusions deprive me
of the full potential of my things,
sailing my boat as often as I should,
shuttering the place for a spontaneous trip –
we give more dinner parties now, invite
boring, trusted friends to look around.

[15]

On the phone to clients, or across
a dealing room's array of desks, the way
you speak does not brook disagreement
– a patois of mutters and twangs.
Adjusting to home, tense still from
breasting the dense atmosphere of work,
it takes so little to set off a row.
One misplaced word and the avalanche
begins: a hail shower of rocks, ropes
failing to grip, your wife as an
ice-maiden throwing glacial looks.

[16]

Reversing into the designated slot
outside your duplex, leaping from
the doeskin seat of a power-steered car,
you feel your life has turned
up trumps; and there are always
further heights to aim for:
set up a consultancy, join the board,
be head-hunted by the rival firm...
You are groomed for better things,
well-positioned in promotion stakes,
dogged, uncompromising and still young.

[17]

The peace of Friday evenings after
staff have left the open-plan deserted,
before cleaners key-in for their shift.
Sun flakes out on the carpet, rays
highlight staplers, calculators, pens;
phones flop in cradles: Monday will
inaugurate another week, small talk
over instant coffee; new debenture stock...
Meanwhile, suspended between worlds, I drum
on the plastic in-tray, stare down at
the frenzied city, disinclined to budge.

[18]

Women who matter in our lives
– secretaries, wives, one taking on
the other's features in the dark –
adapt their habits to our needs,
shrewd about what should be packed
for the tour of brand distributors,
which calls to allow, how to treat
our moods, our swears: we like our
secretaries efficient, young, breaths
of fresh air, able to laugh off risqué
jokes, remain tight-lipped as wives.

[19]

How much longer will this crystal water
flow, this snow come decked in white,
I wonder, as I pour out bottled spring,
brace myself for questions from the floor
about our new cost-cutting scheme...
Even when I mouth defences of our safety
record – latest filters, monitors in place –
I see my children's scornful faces, rivers
shimmering like metal, aluminium-clear,
quivering with farmed fish, squirming with algae,
grey snow lodging on eroded banks...

[20]

Before the car ascends the parking ramp
at nine, I drop my working wife off
with a ritual, perfunctory peck.
Tuna salad shared for lunch, a quick
check on appointments – we touch base
if schedules permit, save news of
office manoeuvres for our pillow talk...
I glimpse from here the nesting pigeon,
awkward, restless, treading on shells,
then load the spreadsheet's spurt
of ballpark figures, analysing trends.

[21]

In this downward phase of the economic
cycle, I despair of pre-tax growth,
the yield from R & D, lose heart.
Our boardroom's abstract art infuriates me:
dashed-off blobs and squiggles. Trash.
I resent the easy fortunes some make,
smarmy advertising agents in white suits,
that painter flogging half-baked wares
for my likes to feel foolish near.
Time again to clear my desk; nothing achieved,
another bitty, gruelling, inconclusive day.

[22]

A torrential morning; drenched to
the cufflinks, I take calls from staff
complaining of sham ailments, voices
straining to sound hoarse or weak…
I think back like a parent to their
early promise: none of the we-have-
something-on-you vibes I get now
whenever I insist on strictness. Surely
they wouldn't go so far as to expose me,
trawl files to sniff out iffy deals?
All the things, with hindsight, I regret.

[23]

The nightmare prospect of retirement:
those pathetic cretins condemned to wring
every last comma from the morning paper –
Deaths column to For Sale – sparing
the crossword until later, keeping out
of their wives' hair, put to grass,
to mow lawns, lives devoid of contrast,
an onset of golf-fatigue and gloom,
eager to resume dictating vital memos
to that secretary, the one confidante
they trusted, the one sympathetic ear.

[24]

When the air crackles with threats
– disaffected personnel, final
notices, debts, legal proceedings –
I am lucky to be ex-directory
at home; and I lie low at work,
go aground, invariably *in a meeting*
if I'm pursued – other times, however,
need a high profile approach:
smiling as a football sponsor,
lashing the Budget in a trade mag,
lobbying a Minister for grants.

[25]

Valentine's Day attracts delivery men
cupping the rosebud flames that radiate
on desks through cellophane – no black
spots, no thorns: model of a world
where wars are misunderstandings, hate
is due to childhood traumas and will pass...
That people are basically good is agreed
at the canteen tea-break, life as plump
with expectation as the satin card
the postman brings; and love will conquer all
in its glass slipper, right to the final stroke.

[26]

Can a year really have passed since our
last Christmas shindig? Here I am
in the same rut, not a single resolution
carried through, deluding myself that
I'm still in my prime. Yes, it's that
time again: a factitious peace, a ceasefire
between camps, an ambience as sweet
as fake rot on marzipan fruits doled out
from desk to desk; tomorrow's gossip will
concern the boss who'll traipse in late,
suit crumpled, mood untypically mute.

[27]

The original sin of officialdom, guilt
we share in secret: mileage rigged,
spare parts purloined, fax used
to conserve sports club cash, things
troubling when the accounts branch
dreams up dodgy questions; taxmen, too,
the nightmare of close scrutiny
– receipts, excuses, bank statements
to prepare – and the attendant dread
of lay-offs, sackings, three-day weeks,
gaunt, haunting figures begging change.

[28]

Then the time comes when you know
none of your promise will be fulfilled;
the saving roles luck, fame, deliverance
from your job were meant to play...
You will slave on till pension day,
eluded by advancement, satisfaction, wealth.
In your head, some plangent melody repeats;
in your mind's eye, a preview of your part
as walk-on stoic, accepting failure in good
heart, battling home against the wind
this night the same as the last.

[29]

Stepping from the lunchtime bistro,
hitting the wet pedestrian-only streets,
I raise our logoed golf umbrella
for a noncommittal client, before we split.
Through the bad reception of rain
come memories of the kissogram french-maid
disoriented in a downpour near the admin tower:
satins, bows so much at odds with
our stressed concrete, steel; her dainty
hesitations in the storm, a creature dazed
by headlights who starts turning heel.

[30]

A quite ordinary man, but go-ahead,
the sort you wouldn't throw a second glance
at in the street, let alone comment on.
If you happen to meet him, nothing will
cross your mind unless his smirk
dimly recalls someone you once knew...
Though his name won't mean a thing
at present, he is nudging forward, destined
for the top – watch the newsboy hold his
evening paper as he dashes down the steps,
gripping folders, lugging research home.

[31]

The white-cuffed sales rep, guarding
territory, does not add up in the age
of central warehousing; the few we still
keep on are doomed: jaunty, over-groomed men,
sharing jokes and samples at the check-outs,
waiting for a brisk assistant manager
to deign to acknowledge their existence,
counting palettes in a draughty store-room,
raising special offers to eye-level shelves.
Commission in decline, their smiles grow
thin; redundancy will come as no surprise.

[32]

Death, once brushed against,
does not seem in the least
like a stubbly ghost with scythe
reaping dry grass in the graveyard,
but shows up as a brash executive
cutting recklessly across your lane,
lights making eye-contact with yours,
ready to meet head-on as though
by previous appointment; ram your
car horn like a panic button: his
cellular telephone will toll for you.

[33]

Phase Two of our unit, I inspect the site
in hard hat and suit, furled plans
like parchment in my hand: a digger's teeth
grind pebble-crunchy, graveyard-yellow clay,
mud choking my oak-coloured semi-brogues.
Faced with such an earth-shattering foray
– the groundwork where progress is rooted –
I sense the desiccated souls of DIY types,
clawing their way through hardware bargains,
prodding at sprockets, widgets, screws,
figuring out some new useless device.

[34]

Guarding against mistakes at any cost,
I steer clear of the PA – lace
blouse and leather skirt – who seemed
ready to reciprocate my interest;
and I try not to fall for lavish gifts
from pushy, new-to-market IT folk
(tokens of appreciation, normal perks
– hampers, country house weekends –
from regulars are perfectly OK): no
rival jerk will do the dirt on me
in first-round interviews for Chief.

[35]

Out on the open road – sun visor, shades,
a guiding hand, the reassuring buoyancy
of tyres; blues and big-band tapes plug gaps
between troubleshooting client operations.
Everywhere seems miles from everywhere,
conflated landscapes scale the heights
as I check with my secretary by phone
that no shit has hit the HQ fan.
The man at the factory entrance-hut
directs me to the guest zone; I lean
back, grab my linen jacket from its hook.

[36]

Good to hold a stable job in these
recessionary times, friends receiving
letters of regret from the foreign parent,
no golden parachute on offer; yet
tempting just the same to make the break,
venture on a lucrative new challenge.
I scan the vacancies (*self-starter,
forward-thinking, profit-responsible,
independent but committed to group culture*),
conjuring my fate in black and white here,
in terms I can relate to, a dynamic role.

[37]

Scarcely to be acknowledged, even to myself,
days when the very sight of my wall planner
makes me sick, when − instead of tough,
decisive judgements delivered with a quick
peremptory scrawl − I sculpt a paper clip,
chew a ballpoint, gaze at the Alpine calendar.
Suit-coat removed, I scroll through e-mail;
there are press releases to issue, markets
to nail... I must switch back to fast track,
delegate; late again tonight, home to my
sleeping child, a wife's taciturn rebuke.

[38]

Over decades, I have said goodbye
to my retiring colleagues, signed
the sentimental cards slyly passed
around, tossed pounds into collection
envelopes, stared at grey down fringing
a hand that squeezes mine, conveying
as much emotion as it dares betray...
We promise to stay in touch but, of
course, we never do after the hearty
speeches end (tributes, in-jokes from
friends) and they drop out of our cast.

[39]

Walking through the automatic exit,
talking heatedly about the downside
of a greenfield site, I am captivated
by a busker's tune: untainted, pure,
drawn from the rainswept mountainy mind
of an old man counting yearlings in the wind,
the log-shifting silence of his hearth...
That music keeps its nerve, unfazed
by the pressing business of the streets;
you continue − 'Right?', 'OK?' − but I,
thread lost, can only mumble and concur.

[40]

First day at the new firm, you treat
warily the insiders you've beaten;
too soon yet to know whose blitheness
camouflages venom. Left to yourself,
taking stock of your plush room, shocked
at the capacious desk-space you must fill,
you speed-read through the introductory
pack (staff pyramids, pie charts, stats)
and worry that — pressures of moving,
children's distress, apart — you may
have misjudged; money isn't everything.

[41]

Like some class of transsexual,
inhabiting the wrong body, you are
trapped in an ungratifying job,
losing self-esteem, but anxious
nonetheless to come plausibly across
as a motivated member of the team;
or is it an out-of-body experience,
so this isn't really you, a goal-
driven executive, setting fresh
parameters, laying down ground rules,
projections tripping off your tongue?

[42]

Creased with the pain of a piercing
duodenal, my thoughts drift to dead
comrades: I pick up from where they
left off, collapsing at a bus stop,
succumbing to a heart attack in bed,
and cut one free of his supportive rope...
Each funeral, my resolution was to listen
to staff problems but the real world
does not, alas, allow for much indulgence:
death-in-service pensions are the extent
of my role, lump sums for next-of-kin.

[43]

The flimsiness of steep buildings,
scintillant ice palaces of glass;
sun-spots, structures opposite are
mirrored, warped; filing cabinets,
work stations, rubber plants in tubs
prove amenable to public scrutiny.
It is like walking on air, the sheer
vertiginous layers of stacked light;
lifts surge through molten floors
or plunge to solidities of sculpted bronze,
revolving doors, terrazzo, guards.

[44]

A monumentally awful day, shopfloor staff
baying for your blood; sighs, grumbles,
union officials clamouring for talks...
Then the recriminations taking you aback:
like a drowning life, your past is
brandished on the far side of the desk,
your certainty about the fairness
of the way you run the branch is challenged,
old feuds reopen and, with tension high,
you still maintain control, adopt a mild,
sincere tone, just as the books advise.

[45]

A Sunday walk: bees nuzzling perennials,
something stirring under roadside furze.
I seldom find time to take in the view
that cost a hefty premium when I invested
in my prime-location home. I know what
umpteen fishing flies, horse trainers,
software packages – you name it – are called,
but not what this wilderness contains
before planning applications sweep it
all away – motor mowers blazing trails
to a culture of microwaves, antiques.

[46]

Not afraid of risks, not listening to
cagey advice; striking out from time
to time, irrespective of whose toes
you're forced to tread on – whatever's
needed to bring your plans on-stream.
However tight the ship, there will always
be some weak links in line management:
bypass them, oblige the shirkers
to shape up or go – any fallout from your
hardline approach may be made good in
due course; meanwhile, stand your ground.

[47]

All the profitless minutes I expend
on matters not recorded in my timesheet.
The clients' fees (so much per hour
plus VAT) should be reduced to take
account of idle daydreams: hotel trysts
with that ravishing sophisticate
from payroll, sneaking off towards
the border in twin bucket seats…
Jolted back from perfumes, limbs
– or thoughts of league scores, injured
props – I continue with put options, liens.

[48]

You could do it in your sleep, the dawn
trek through another empty terminal,
vinyl undergoing a mechanical shine,
gift shops shut – cigars, frilled silk
behind steel grilles – bales of early
papers bursting to blurt out their news…
Fanning stale air with your boarding pass,
if you look up from your business-class recliner
during the safety drill, it will be only
to eyeball the stewardess; you itch
to switch your laptop on, rejig the unit price.

[49]

Some networking is necessary to get
to the right people, turning on the charm,
having them eat out of your palm, but never
put entirely on the spot, everything off
the record, a once-only concession you
won't mention to your friends, strictly
between yourselves, without prejudice...
Futile dealing with less senior staff,
sticklers for detail, holding progress back.
At clubs, committees, conferences, make a point
of banging heads together, picking brains.

[50]

Halogen lights tested, alarm code set,
I burrow into the high-tog, duckdown quilt;
the number-crunching radio-clock squanders
digital minutes like there was no tomorrow.
Who will remember my achievements when
age censors me from headed notepaper?
Sometimes, if I try to pray, it is with
dead colleagues that I find myself communing...
At the end of the day, for my successors too,
what will cost sleep are market forces, vagaries
of share price, p/e ratio, the bottom line.

New and Recent Poetry from Anvil

TONY CONNOR
Metamorphic Adventures

PETER DALE
Edge to Edge
NEW AND SELECTED POEMS

DICK DAVIS
Touchwood

DICK DAVIS
Borrowed Ware
MEDIEVAL PERSIAN EPIGRAMS

JAMES HARPUR
The Monk's Dream

ANTHONY HOWELL
First Time in Japan

IVAN V. LALIĆ
Fading Contact
TRANSLATED BY FRANCIS R. JONES

PETER LEVI
Reed Music

THOMAS McCARTHY
The Lost Province

VASKO POPA
Collected Poems
TRANSLATED BY ANNE PENNINGTON & FRANCIS R. JONES

SALLY PURCELL
Fossil Unicorn

PETER RUSSELL
The Elegies of Quintilius

RUTH SILCOCK
A Wonderful View of the Sea

A catalogue of our publications is available on request